7 BEST SACRIFICES TO SUCCESS

A Productive Book to Boost Confidence, Enhance Self-Belief, Build Success Mindset and Become Mega Successful in Life.

PRADIP N DAS

Table of Content

Introduction

"Human progress is neither automatic nor inevitable... Every step toward the goal of justice requires sacrifice, suffering, and struggle; the tireless exertions and passionate concern of dedicated individuals."
– Martin Luther King Jr.

The United States of America's famous President Abraham Lincoln was born in a log cabin in the forest. He grew up in a very poor family in Kentucky and Indiana. He could not afford a lamp and read borrowed books with the light of the fire in the hearth. He was self-educated and merely by working hard, he became the greatest man of his time. All great achievers such as Nelson Mandela, Mahatma Gandhi, Steve Jobs, Dr. Abdul Kalam, Elon Musk, etc. worked very hard, burnt midnight oil, showed extreme perseverance, and sacrificed many things before they became successful.

Success is not easy. It is more difficult for bigger success. People encounter many challenges throughout the journey of success and face various uncomfortable and turbulent situations. Success does not have one point solution. It is pure passion, learning, actions, hard work, perseverance, sacrifice, self-belief, etc., and above all the degree of desperation to achieve success. To become successful, one needs to invest enormous amounts of time in reading, learning, and experimenting.

Sacrifice is one of the most important elements in success. People desire many things in life but very few are ready to sacrifices for that. Those who want to lose weight do not want to sacrifice lavish foods, people who desire to improve fitness do not want to go to the gymnasium for fitness training regularly, students who aspire to make a great career do not want to learn the required knowledge and skills.

The bigger the sacrifices, the bigger the success. Success requires sacrifice, one should be ready to pay the price for success. Many changes occur in the mind of the person during sacrifices. A lot of challenges are encountered and many stressful situations are faced during this testing time.

But the positive thing is that, during this after sacrificing, the level of grit and determination increases manifold there are a lot of things are at stake, people have no other options but to focus on the work for achieving the goals and try to put all resources towards achieving the goal only. Thereby, sacrifices are directly proportional to improvement in determination, willpower, focus, hard work, discipline, and many more aspects of achieving the goal. Similarly, the willingness to sacrifice directly determines your level of success. If you truly want to reach another level of success in any area of your life, you will need to make extraordinary sacrifices to reach there. Sacrifices can be in the form of time, money, resources, enjoyment, sleep, social life, etc. Parents sacrifice everything for their children, in some cases, they even sacrifice precious time and career for their child to support for their career. These sacrifices are essential for success. A successful career requires dedication and if people are not willing to make sacrifices in life for their career, for their future, then they never reach that success.

What Makes Person Successful?

Every individual in this world wants to become successful, everyone wants a successful luxurious life but wanting success will not give you a successful life. Success does not come to anyone, instead, people go towards a successful journey. There is a huge difference between successful people and unsuccessful people. Successful people never take success journey leniently. They know that anything worth never comes easy, Success is not as easy as unsuccessful people think. Successful people know that when you want something from life then you need to sacrifice something for it. Without sacrificing something in life nobody can reach the peak of success.

Successful people get success because they work hard for it, they sacrifice a lot for that success. Success needs Sacrifice means life demands something in return to give you success. Success is something which you earn, which you achieve by your hard work after a lot of sacrifices.

The biggest problem of unsuccessful people is that they want to succeed but by not doing hard work and by staying in the comfort zone. Studies find that unsuccessful people want everything readymade. They do not want to put in efforts, they lack persistence and want to play safe always. They are not risk-takers. They want it free of cost. These never allow them to become successful.

Success is a part of life. It is something to aspire to. Successful people get success because they work hard for it, they never ask for success. They get it because they deserve it, they sacrifice a lot for that success. Hence if you are willing to do the necessary sacrifices for success then you will move towards the success journey. Additionally, you need to put in your 100 percent or more than 100 percent efforts and should have never given up attitude, etc. which will take you towards the success journey.

Why Sacrifices Necessary to Success?

According to Oxford Dictionaries, a sacrifice is an act of giving up something valued for the sake of something else regarded as more important or worthy.

American author, Napoleon Hill said, "Great achievement is usually born of great sacrifice, and is never the result of selfishness." Thus, to achieve goals and dreams successfully, one needs to willingly sacrifice many things in one's life no matter if they are big or small. There will be many hardships and trials along the journey to success. A successful man is prepared to sacrifice his time, money, power, energy, self-interest and personal belongings, and even life for the achievement of success.

Many people are simply not willing to give up their short-term pleasures for higher-level long-term pleasures. They are lost in the moment and simply unable to bear through periods of short-term pain that they must get through to experience ultimate pleasure in the future.

If you're serious about attaining your desired objectives, then you must be willing to let go of the small pleasures found at the moment that might very well distract and sabotage you from living the ultimate long-term pleasures that you will experience once your goal has been achieved.

We must know that to gain success in whatever we want to do, sacrificing should be one of the keys to victory. Learning swimming without practicing daily or even get rich without working hard – is never possible. Success is not so cheap, there is always some price to pay for that.

The Consequences of Making No Sacrifices

The goals and objectives you have in mind will not be automatically fulfilled in your life. You will need to work very hard consistently over some time and make huge sacrifices along the way to achieve your goals. When you sacrifice something in life, it prevents you to procrastinate, helps you to make decisions and take actions, it forces you to persevere and try again and again. When these things happen to you, you automatically move towards your goal. By making sacrifices, you take responsibility for your life to become successful desperately and make a commitment to making your life better.

Sacrifice typically means giving something up of value to get something even more valuable in the future. The people in the world who achieve the most are the ones who can sacrifice. It is a pure trade. You need to understand that when you give something then only you will get something. Giving something up could come in the form of your hard work time, energy, or money. You might need to sacrifice one of these things, or maybe a combination of these things to become successful.

One of the greatest causes of failure in life is the inability to make sacrifices. The power of sacrifice is something that can change lives and has huge meaning.

Types of Sacrifices

Sacrifices are made all the time. People sacrifice for the Nation, religion, your society, family, siblings, children, friends, profession, arts, science, nature, love, and in everyday life. A sacrifice is made when someone gives up something that they value, for the sake of something more important. It could be a sacrifice as big as your life, or just sacrificing a few hours of sleep to get work done. Parents make sacrifices for their children all the time. Children make similar sacrifices for their families as well. Like not hanging out with their friends to spend more time with the family instead. Sacrificing means prioritizing your focus for some things leaving all others aside to achieve something. If you want to sacrifice your life for your parents you can do so by becoming a better child, de-prioritizing all your requirements.

If you want to sacrifice life for your family, you can try to become a better person and give them the love and necessity they want. Giving them the time they want and listening to them when they need you.

If you want to sacrifice your life for the country, you can try to become a better citizen, contribute to the nations in some way, preserve the nation's heritage and assets, follow the rules and pay the taxes, avoid engaging in wrong practices, etc.

When our soldiers protect our borders to defend the nation, they face tremendous hardship due to rough weather, away from family, sometimes they die. They make supreme sacrifices so that citizens of the nation live a normal life.

We have seen that in families, due to some situation, some family members, the elder son or elder daughter or uncle has to make a sacrifice for meeting the needs of the entire families - including financial needs of the family. Ultimately, they sacrifice their life in the family by depriving them of their education for themselves to meet the financial burden during childhood to feed the family members.

In a society too, people sometimes sacrifice many of their comforts for meeting others' needs.

Impact of Sacrifices

"Anything that you cannot sacrifice pins you. Makes you predictable, makes you weak." — Mark Lawrence

Every person sacrifices something in life. The level of sacrifice determines the level of success. From my childhood until today, I sacrificed many things in life. Time, energy, entertainment, sleep, family, social relation, and money to name a few. Because while growing up, I was hoping that my sacrifices will yield a better result and they did.

One of the greatest causes of failure in life is the inability to make sacrifices. The power of sacrifice is something that can change lives and has huge meaning. Sacrifice is a must if you want to grow in life. If you study the lives of successful people, you will find different kinds of sacrifices they made in their life. The very common sacrifices are entertainment, time, social life, comfort, family, social life, etc.

If you want to excel in academics, then you have to spend time studying and staying away from social media, because it will eat up your time. If you want to be a world-class sportsperson, then sacrifice your enjoyment with friends and family members, avoid mouthwatering lavish foods, instead, you need to work out in the gymnasium and spend time acquiring skills about that sports. If you want to become an actor, then sacrifice your private life and will have to spend time acquiring skills of acting, dancing, singing, fitness, etc. Sacrifice is the one thing that decides your success in sports and the game of life. Being successful requires sacrificing something, like time, money, or pleasures, so that you can hone your skills and pursue your dreams. Therefore, to succeed at anything in life, you need to sacrifice many things to cut off all distractions and give more time to achieve your goal.

When you learn how to use sacrifice to your advantage, you gain a versatile tool for success for the rest of your life. Dave Ramsey said, "The most important decision about your goals is not what you're willing to do to achieve them, but what you are willing to give up." Are you willing to keep away from social media for your study and career? Are you willing to stay away from oily and spicy foods to be in peak physical health? Are you willing to give up hanging out with friends to prepare for an upcoming tournament? Most people are willing "to do," but very few are willing to "give up." The reality is, if you do not sacrifice for your goals, then you will sacrifice your goals. It is important to remember that the cost of every sacrifice comes with corresponding benefits. Yes, you are giving up some morning sleeping time to do extra conditioning, but you are gaining a higher level of physical fitness and a better chance of winning the next game. Sports create a culture that drives and encourages the "sacrifice required" mentality.

Benefits of Sacrificing

The main purpose of making sacrifices is not to cause suffering, instead, it is to achieve goals or to alleviate long-term suffering.

Success is connected to doing things that are not fun for the moment. It is connected to channeling your energy into completing that task that gives you agony and lack of enjoyment.

The word sacrifice seems to have negative connotations, but in many senses that it is not correct. Sacrifice is often about prioritization and discipline since we do not always have space or time in our lives to accommodate all the things we would like. You have got to lose some to gain some.

However, the benefits of sacrifices are many:-

- Sacrifice helps you to take charge of your life making you responsible for your actions
- Sacrifice builds character, makes you down to earth, changes behavior and attitude, and makes yourself better.
- It strengthens willpower and determination, empowers you to make decisions, and fulfillment.
- It can make you serious about your goal, more discipline, and improve your maturity.
- Sacrifice increases one's self-control.
- If you sacrifice today you will be paid off with interest sooner or later.
- Sacrifice teaches us how powerful our minds can be when we put our minds to something.

- Sacrifice builds resilience and strengthens mental health, and creates a "never give up" attitude.

The Other Side

Success is connected to doing things that are not fun for the moment. It is connected to channeling your energy into completing that task that gives you agony and lack of enjoyment. Sacrifices can be very tiresome, it can hurt very much. Sacrifice can be a very lonely battle. A sacrifice to be real must cost, must hurt, and must empty ourselves. Sacrifices are never easy. It can be a game of chance where you can either win or lose. Not because you paid the price for something, it does not necessarily mean you will have it. Some external factors beyond your control play an important part in your wishes and sacrifices. Sacrifice at times won't make you happy at that time but in the future, you'll realize that you did right by doing it. However, it may not guarantee sure success.

Sacrifice is important as it is proof that we are not mere talk and no walk. It proves we are serious in that pursuit.

We must exactly know the things that are worth sacrificing and the things which are not. We must clearly understand what we can and cannot sacrifice. What truly matters to us in the long run and would give us lesser regrets and disappointments.

Well, when it comes to sacrifice anything the first thing we should think is what will it cause us in the long run though sacrifices are important in life because it teaches us that how to live without the things we need most in our life. Sometimes we have to let go off things, but the reality behind sacrifices is that what do you think about that person from your heart. It's not always for one or for the people we know but also for those who when we see and feel that he or she need more of me then and there. People do not always leave for selfish motives but because there was no reason for them to stay in your life. There will be times when you will feel alone or that you are left with an empty hand just remember if have done anything good for someone, God has his way to get you out of it as they. So it is not necessary but good to make sacrifices in your life.

Every single human being wants to succeed at something. Whether it be sports, school, their job, or even the overall concept of life. They want to do what their peers did wrong. What does this entail? This demands that they sacrifice some concept of freedom to succeed. Sacrifice is more important than success because one cannot achieve success without sacrificing something first. If a student wants to get an A on their test, they need to sacrifice time from their day to study. If a soldier wants to be a hero, they must sacrifice their family, their honor, and even their life. Throughout Earth's history, there have been many records of heroic deeds, depicting what they did to succeed. In each of these stories, it tells the reader what they have to give up to receive. Nothing will happen if the hero does not attempt to make a change.

Chapter Summary

We often waste a lot of time on tiny pleasures which have a very short impact. We must get over those tiny pleasures to get a bigger one. But when you are truly passionate and desperate to achieve something, those sacrifices won't matter. The return will be more precious.

Sacrifices of Comforts

"Success is no accident. It is hard work, perseverance, learning, studying, sacrifice and most of all, love of what you are doing or learning to do." – Pele.

At age 24 years, Elon Musk co-founded a software company called Zip2. The company rapidly grew to support clients and then sold to Compaq for more than $300M. When he was 28 years, he had already made $22 million from the sale of his first company. Musk could have chosen a comfortable life for the rest of his life. But, he did not do that. Musk invested $10M from the sale of his company to get x.com, which became PayPal later on by merger. He sold PayPal just after 3 years to eBay for $1.5 billion. From $22 million at the age of 28 years, he amassed a net worth of $175 million at age 31 years.

But that was just the beginning. Even before PayPal was sold, Musk had already founded SpaceX with $100 million of his own money. The vision behind SpaceX was simple, he could cut the costs of space travel by orders of magnitude, and in the process revitalize space exploration by using new technologies and approaches. Today, SpaceX has achieved a long list of firsts in the space industry. It is the only private company to dock at the international space station, as well as the only private company to return a spacecraft from low orbit. It has also created some of the most powerful space rockets in the world. Being a pioneer in space travel is hard, it's uncomfortable, but it's just a part-time job for Elon Musk.

To gain something, the first-person needs to come out of the very painful comfort zone. Many people love to live inside their comfort zone, which let them miss so many opportunities in life. But, successful people do not prefer to live inside the comfort zone. They challenge themselves so that they can reach the peak of their performance and deliver their best.

Your comfort zone is a dangerous place. It prevents you from improving, it stops you from achieving all the things you are capable of achieving and it makes your life miserable in the future. Once you move out of your comfort zone, you are naturally going to achieve more than ever before. Because of your alertness and increased concentration and focus, you will develop new skills. Those new skills will change the way you see yourself, encouraging you to step even further out of your comfort zone.

Stepping out of your comfort zone always brings up some fear of the unknown. There is always a certain level of uncertainty when we push ourselves. But it is required to break the shackle of routine and go out of my comfort zone to overcome feeling the fear.

The Comfort Zone is Nothing But a Cage

People believe that the comfort zone is when they are at ease, experience low or free from stress or anxiety, same routine work, no challenges, no uncertainty. Comfort zones vary from person to person because different people have different anxiety and stress levels, diverse mindsets, and different tolerance levels.

Therefore, the comfort zone would be a state of mind where a person's anxiety. For example, some people love to go to work every morning and they enjoy daily routine works and become their comfort zone and leaving this comfort zone to become a freelancer or start a business can be very challenging for them. For others, the comfort zone may be extended sleep in the morning or just a steady flow of income from a secured job. Some may feel a comfort zone could be the siesta, when they relax in front of the television, or when listening to music. Comfort zones are dynamic and keep on changing based on the time and situation of your life you feel most comfortable with. People feel comfortable in a certain state, as time passes, they feel anxiety in the same comfort zone due to many personal, professional, internal & external reasons, and ultimately it converts into a cage. When you begin to feel vulnerable anxious, stressed, uncomfortable about doing something, then you are stepping out of your comfort zone or you are faced with the threat of stepping outside your comfort zone.

Why People Prefer to Stay in the Comfort Zone?

There are plenty of reasons to live within your comfort zone. You feel safe, secure, and confident with minimal stress and anxiety. You have already accustomed to the work you are doing, even the challenges are also routine, and you can predict what is coming next.

A lot of people do not want to risk taking chances in life, even though they are bored of being in the comfort zone. The withholding factors could be many such as family responsibilities, the fear of failure, lack of confidence, fear of the unknown, etc. When you tackle familiar tasks in your comfort zone, you are aware of the risks and know how to avoid them. Familiar activities tend to be less risky than unknown ones. The reason people stay in their comfort zones relates to the fact that people are naturally risk-averse.

When we see uncertainty, we view it negatively. We assume first that bad things will happen if we go outside of our comfort zone, rather than good things will happen. Statistically, this is not true; it is more likely a 50/50 in most cases.

Psychologically this is not true either, as both success and failures in new areas grow our mindset and neural process.

Also for some people, the case is that they do not wish to venture out into unknown territory because they underestimate themselves. If an activity is in your comfort zone, chances are you can complete it quickly and easily without too much forethought or planning. The ease of routine tasks frees up more time and mental energy for addressing challenging work.

When you choose to stay in your comfort zone, you participate in familiar activities. You perform tasks you have completed repeatedly, and likely with a track record of success. Staying in your comfort zone allows you to draw on experience you have gained from past performances, in areas you undoubtedly know well. The advantage of the comfort zone is safety and stability, but it comes at a cost. The cost for remaining in the comfort zone is growth. In other words, if we become too comfortable, we probably are not learning and growing. I think there is even a saying- "there is no growth in the comfort zone."

They do not believe that they might just make it through. Also, when they see the struggle others go through to achieve something in life, they are scared of the struggle without even look for the achievement part.

Without a doubt, there are convincing reasons to spend time in your comfort zone. For people who do move out of their comfort zones, this can be one of two things. First, it could be that this person is naturally risk-seeking, in which case they don't follow the general risk-averse public. These types of people are naturally rare, but they do exist. More often, they are risk-averse people who have simply learned that they will have better growth if they continuously go outside the comfort zone.

Why Comfort Zone Is The Main Impediment to Success

Most people never try to come out of their comfort zone as long as they do feel any stress, vulnerability, or threats resulting in they do not experiment with new things and are deprived of new learnings. The implications are many by staying in the comfort zone.

- Stops personal growth

When you are staying in your comfort zone for a longer time, you will always at the same level of knowledge and skills, never moving forward and never growing. Most people who love to stay in their comfort zones usually fail to achieve their goals because they are somewhat obsessed with doing things the same way they have always done them even when it is not producing results. As a result, people fail to explore their potential and limits. The challenges and urge to learn something new are absent, new learning does not happen, personal development automatically stops there.

- Diminish in motivational level

When people stay longer time in the comfort zone, their mindset and vision become very narrow and they stop thinking about goals and purpose resulting in a huge drop in motivation in life.

- Sharp decline of passion

It is difficult to discover passion when people are in the cage of their comfort zone. This can only be found by stepping away from comfort zone. If you are not where you want to be in your life, it may be because you are stuck inside of your comfort zone.

It is easy to do what you are used to doing and staying within the confines of least resistance, but if you want to make progress in your life, you need to break free from what holds you back.

- Impaired mindset

It is hard to see a positive mindset if a person lives in a comfort zone for longer life. They always see the negative part first and in a bigger way. Because of looking at the negative part in a magnifying glass, the positive aspects are covered up.

Why People Should Come Out of Their Comfort Zone?

Needless to say that people who wish to get success in their comfort zone, actually never want their dream to come true, they are living in a fool's paradise. A Comfort zone is a nice place, but nothing ever grows there. Therefore, if you want to be successful and if you consider success more important, then you will never settle yourself in your comfort zone. Successful people take risks, move out of their comfort zone, take every possible step to get what they want. They explore new things and go above their limits. They want success they never wish for it, hence to be successful you need to sacrifice your comfort zone.

To function effectively in this rapidly changing world, you need to learn new things to remain in the fray. Lifelong learning will help you to adapt to all changes. By continuing to learn, you will more easily step out of your comfort zone and will grow in your career.

Besides, learning new things gives you a feeling of accomplishment which, in turn, boosts confidence in your capabilities, gets rid of "fear of the unknown", and takes charge of your own life more easily to succeed.

How to Leave Comfort Zone

- It takes courage to step outside of your comfort zone and face your fears head-on. After all, there is no guarantee that the risks you will take will turn out the way you want.

- Courage is developed in many ways, like taking actions, taking calculated risks, keeping in uncomfortable positions, making mistakes.

- If a person keeps taking action, he can anticipate the consequences; he can take a calculated risk, accept failures, accept changes. It brings a lot of pain and discomfort to the person but gradually develops all the qualities required for success, including courage.

- Varying influences such as parents, peers, siblings, etc. contribute in your life to shaping and conditioning your comfort zone. You have to overcome these influences and the conditions that have shaped the boundaries of your comfort zone.

- You need to change your habits and behaviors that relate to your comfort zone. You cannot just do these overnight, you have to slowly push yourself out of your comfort zone and expand it.

- If the fear of failure holds us back from exploring our options and getting out of our comfort zones, then you allow yourself to fail in small things. Once you are accustomed to failing, you have nothing left to fear anymore. You become unafraid to take risks and get out of your comfort zone to achieve everything you want.

- Many top performers find ways to push themselves and to come out of the comfort zone frequently. This helps to lay a good foundation for mental wellness. There is no more excellent teacher of confidence than to see yourself do something you avoided before.

Chapter Summary

Although your comfort zone might be the most comfortable part of your life, it is not wise to stay locked in it as it will not allow you to be who you are capable of being. And, most certainly, your big dreams and goals won't come to pass so you need to work for them, and you can't do that from your comfort zone.

Fear of insecurity is very common in the human mind which always tries to tell you that to not to go for any change or any uncertainty. It defends this.

Sacrifices of Entertainment

"The trouble is, you think you have time."
—Jack Kornfield

We live in the era of the internet, you can have immediate fulfillment. If you want to watch a movie, just open Netflix, if you want any mouthwatering foods, just order online, will be delivered in no time. If you want to see what your friends are up to, just send a message and see a quick update on Facebook or Instagram. One can usually gratify one's desires in just a few minutes. Achieving anything notable takes time. When you are accustomed to instant fulfillment, your patience level drops drastically. Due to this, you feel frustrated when your goals do not achieve quickly.

Many people have developed the habit of watching TV serials every evening or watch sports for hours or watching youtube videos at late night. Many children are so addicted to cartoons and video games, they can't live for a moment without this and their parents also surrendered to their demands. Some people are busy on Twitter or Instagram or Facebook throughout the day, keep on engaging themselves on likes, comments, and shares. Some of them are either surrender their life and just enjoy life as it is. They enjoy the present moment, don't bother about taking any new challenges on their own and about the future. Their lives have been completely taken over by social media or similar things unconsciously.

Whether your hobby is playing piano, playing chess, or social networking, if it consumes too much of your time and distracts you from your goal, then you have to let them go, at least for time being. Now if your hobby is one of those things that is a stress reliever after a long week of work, that is fine, but if you are out to enjoy chit-chatting with your friends every day in the evening at the cost of your valuable work, that is unacceptable in these circumstances. You need to take things this way—it is always a better choice to sacrifice today's fun for prosperous tomorrow.

Why Sacrifice Entertainment

Successful people do sacrifice now for something better later. For instance, a swimmer starts practicing swimming at 5.00 a.m. throughout the year, when their friends are still in bed. He gives up sleep to win the championship next year. The sacrifice of present pleasure is indispensable to have a great life in the future. If a person has learned to sacrifice comfort and short-term pleasure and can apply it to their life, they will excel in life.

Belarusian-American entrepreneur, author, speaker, and Internet personality Gary Vaynerchuk says, "I've learned the importance of sacrificing short-term pleasures for long-term happiness. Life is a long game, and when you start a business, you've made a decision that doesn't allow any time in year one to focus on anything but building it. I'm talking code red, 18-hours-a-day dedicated...But in two or three years, when I'm taking my kids on business trips and showing them the world, we're reaping the benefits."

In other words, delay in gratification is the act of resisting an impulse to take an immediately available reward in the hope of obtaining a more-valued reward in the future. The ability to delay gratification indicates self-regulation and self-control. Choosing a long-term reward over immediate gratification poses a significant challenge in many areas of life.

Instant and delayed are the two branches of gratification. People who look for instant gratification focus on the present. These people are not able to have control over their inclinations and are prone to temptations. People who search for delayed gratification will wait for the future. They maximize their pleasure by looking forward to the anticipated reward. Jake Kelfer, author and an inspirational speaker, simplified the terms by saying instant gratification is fast food on the way home. In contrast, delayed gratification is waiting to have healthier food at home, leading to a healthier and better lifestyle. In financial language, instant gratification is getting a cash advance on a credit card. Delayed gratification is investing in mutual bonds.

Delay in gratification improves one's problem-solving skills, willpower, and ability to reach goals faster. It makes a person optimistic and resilient and teaches the benefits of hard work. Delayed gratification reinforces the value of your work. It gives self–motivation and leads to greater success in life. It improves mental health and helps to improve healthy habits. Delayed gratification has become the most compelling trait of successful people. According to Aristotle, true happiness entails delaying pleasure. A life of purpose, aligned with the seeking of true happiness, creates real joy. It keeps one's happiness meter pretty steady throughout one's life.

How to Resist or Sacrifice the Temptation?

Are you ready to put WhatsApp, Facebook, and Instagram on hold? Are you willing to give up Saturdays at the movies and focus on work? Are you prepared to leave comfort to put in long hours and burn the midnight oil? Are you mentally prepared to leave gossiping with friends in the evening at parks? It will be difficult but it will be worth it.

It is difficult but not impossible. This barrier of temptation can be broken by finding out your passion and the purpose of your life and check whether the goal is aligned to the purpose or not. You need to understand what you want. You will be able to sacrifice all these temporary gratifications only if your purpose or why is stronger than anything else. Revisiting of purpose and WHY should be visualized daily, reviewed periodically, and strengthened by creating emotional attachments. If this happens, you automatically leave everything and go all out to attain the goal.

Chapter Summary

Entertainment is nothing but sweet poison, it eats times very fast, makes people addicted, and then it is impossible to get out of that situation and forced people to succumb. Success requires doing things that do not give momentary pleasure but benefit us in the long run. It requires hard work, the sacrifice of all current pleasures, and a lot of perseverance. If you can master that, you will experience an abundance of success.

Sacrifice of Social Life

"Follow your passion, be prepared to work hard and sacrifice, and, above all, don't let anyone limit your dreams."
- Donovan Bailey

Grant Cardone, New York Times best-selling author of "Be Obsessed or Be Average" and top sales expert who has built a $500 million real estate empire, said, "Before 2008, I was playing golf three times a week. I got distracted and entitled, started to rest on my laurels, and put my family at risk. I decided to master my work and money; if my golf game or social status suffered, so be it. It's OK to sacrifice fun today for freedom tomorrow. I sacrifice every day, doing the things I might not want to do, but doing them anyway for a better future."

Good Social Life - The Anti-Catalyst to Success

Human beings are social by nature and are considered an important part of society and human life. Each one of us desires to have a social community and fruitful social life to stay happy and connected to share knowledge, build up social skills, become famous in the friend circle, and get recognized in the family and society at large. This helps to become cheerful, accomplishment to a certain degree, reduce anxiety levels, etc.

But sometimes there are bigger concerns if you look at holistically. Every individual on this planet wants to get successful, wants a successful luxurious life but wanting success will not give you a successful life. If you believe that success comes to only so-called lucky or rich people then your belief is just a myth. Success never comes to anyone, instead, people go towards a "success journey." As everyone's goal in life is to be successful in some way, most try to attain this through a career. A successful career brings reputation in society, improves financial capability, and sustains their life journey. With everything, success brings there is something that has to be given up or set aside. Just mere enjoying social life does not make the person successful, instead, they end up becoming mediocre only.

Many examples in the success people, they do not have time to hang out with friends and socialize. You might need to end some of your close friendships that is the price to pay for their success. You may not have a social life at all. Sacrifice happens throughout life. The most painful sacrifices at the early age of life are to away from a friend to hang out, to go to a movie or enjoy a party with friends, or stay in the hostel away from parents. At that particular time, it makes more sense for you to focus on education or any other goals you have leaving the momentary enjoyment aside.

To succeed in life, particularly in entrepreneurship, one important thing to sacrifice is some social, professional, and family relationships. If you do not sacrifice these, it will not let you focus on your present work making difficulties in overcoming challenges. This is true that as you go up the ladder of success, your circle and friends and relationships get narrower.

Entrepreneurs often fail to give attention to the family members and their needs, miss playing with their children, not able to help their kids to do homework, fail to attend birthday parties of friends and family members, fails to support during challenging times in the family, miss parent-teacher meetings at the school and even wedding anniversaries. Successful entrepreneurs make priorities in their life and they stick to those priorities treating all other matters as trivial and sacrifice those even it is family & social life.

Sacrifice is always difficult, painful, and lingering. The main impediment is that you will receive pieces of advice, comments from family, friends, seniors, juniors, and society at large causing stress and make things more complicated. Many people sacrifice social life to become successful. For introverted people, it is not so difficult to sacrifice a social life, but for an extrovert, it is one of the hardest things to do. But they even do that for their better future.

What Can be Done?

Social life should be curbed. But that does not mean that you will be completely detached from friends, family, and society. You can keep in touch with your close friends and family from time to time, but completely away from those regular meetings in the evening and weekends with friends and other socializing which consume a lot of your valuable time and distract you from your goal. You can continue things that do not adversely affect your productivity rather than improve your productivity by refreshing and recharging you so that you can work full of energy. But the things to avoid are:-

- Stop weekend enjoyment - You can enjoy visiting someplace on one of the weekends or can do some refreshing work occasionally but making a routine to go out every weekend and spend long hours must be stopped.

- Late-night unproductive work - Proper sound sleep should be ensured to remain productive the next day. Late-night movies with family members or engage in unproductive work disturb the body clock and reduce productivity drastically.

- Avoid partying with friends for long hours - Frequent partying with friends, colleagues, and others takes your focus out from your goals. This should be strictly avoided to remain on the growth track.

- Stop using social networks – Many people are active in social media to remain attached to their friends and family members who stay away from them. In that case, you can allocate a fixed time for social networking and mindless web browsing and strictly adhere to this allocation time. You better stop social networking completely if you are doing it for pleasure only because times are rapidly consumed in social networking without any productive work.

Chapter Summary

In short, to become successful in life or business, a person would have to put a curb on social life, spend lesser time with close members of the family. But this is the general rule of nature. Sacrificing social life at least for time being is a must for success.

Sacrifice of Multi-tasking

"You will never reach your destination if you stop and throw stones at every dog that barks." —Winston S. Churchill

You often find that people do listening to music while exercising or cooking dinner while talking on the phone or holding a conversation while driving.

Multitasking seems like a great way to get a lot done at once. But research has shown that our brains are not nearly as good at handling multiple tasks as we think. Some researchers suggest that multitasking can reduce productivity by as much as 40%. If you are convinced that multitasking makes you super-productive, you are wrong. By multitasking, you switching one task after another frequently, and because every time you switch tasks, you have to repeat a bit to find out where you last left off.

Multitasking reduces your efficiency and performance because your brain can only focus on one thing at a time. When you try to do two things at once, your brain cannot perform both tasks successfully as the brain takes time to refocus one task after another.

A study by Stanford researchers found the brains of multitaskers work less efficiently even when they are not multitasking. Research also shows that, in addition to slowing you down, multitasking lowers your IQ. Several studies have shown that high multitaskers experience greater problems focusing on important and complicated tasks, memory impairment of new subject matter, difficulty learning new materials, and increased stress levels.

If you are doing several different things at once, then you may be what researchers refer to as a "heavy multitasker." You probably think that you are fairly good at this balancing act. According to several studies, however, you are probably not as effective as you think you are.

Research

In a 2010 study, Harvard psychologists Matthew Killingsworth and Daniel Gilbert found that people spend almost 47% of their waking hours thinking about something other than what they are currently doing.

The simple fact that multitasking takes more energy than single-tasking has compounding effects. Suddenly, because your attention is elsewhere, simple tasks take longer than they should, resulting in a delay in the daily schedule and stressing out because you fall behind.

When you fully focus on a single task, you are more likely to get in a state of flow, feel less stress, and enjoy the work you are doing.

Research has demonstrated that that switching from one task to the next takes a serious toll on productivity. Multitaskers have more trouble tuning out distractions than people who focus on one task at a time. Also, doing so many different things at once can impair cognitive ability. To determine the impact of multitasking, psychologists asked study participants to switch tasks and then measured how much time was lost by switching.

Some researchers suggest that productivity can be reduced by as much as 40% by the mental blocks created when people switch tasks. Now it is understood the potential detrimental impact of multitasking, you can put this knowledge to work to increase your productivity and efficiency.

The next time you find yourself multitasking when you are trying to be productive, take a quick assessment of the various things you are trying to accomplish. Eliminate distractions and try to focus on one task at a time.

Drawbacks of Multitasking

Our competitive business world has encouraged multitasking for years. Recent studies, however, show that constant multitasking results in decreased focus, memory and learning impairment, and an increase in stress levels. Multitasking can have other negative effects.

Since students are not giving their full attention to their schoolwork, they are not as effective at absorbing the information they are studying. Longer and more frequent distractions from multitasking can cause school performance to drop even more.

Successful people know this. That is why they choose one thing and then beat it into submission. Being fully present and committed to one task, is indispensable.

- A sharp decline in focus and learning. During multitasking, your mind is never really focused on any one task. In a study published in the US National Library of Medicine, researchers determined that heavy media multitaskers are more susceptible to distractions from irrelevant stimuli, resulting in greater problems focusing on important tasks. Because our minds are distracted and are unable to process or retain that new information. This inability to concentrate can impact your professional life but also has implications on personal experiences and relationships.

- When doing several things at once, your mind is divided between them so it is only natural that your mistakes will multiply. And according to Stanford research, multitaskers are terrible at filtering out irrelevant information.

- Creativity is inhibited. Devoting your attention to too many tasks at once, you will never come up with new creative ideas and concepts. Probably, you will be able to fulfill your routine works done at a moderate rate and scope, but greatness will be beyond your reach.

- A major downside of multitasking is the increasing level of anxiety that plagues people who consistently divide their attention. A study conducted by researchers at the University of California, where they performed a test that measured the heart rates of employees with and without access to office email. Those who could access their emails remained wired up – they exhibited higher heart rates than those who didn't have access. On the other hand, the second group was observed to perform their jobs relatively stress-free.

- Further studies show a negative physical effect on the body, in addition to a negative cognitive effect. Multitaskers experience a release of stress hormones and adrenaline in the bodies. The result can often become a vicious cycle of constant multitasking, requiring more time to complete a long list of tasks, experiencing high stress.

- When you distractedly attempt to complete small tasks while also trying to complete a large one, you'll soon see how they eat up more of your time rather than saving it. The mind has to reset to each task following the shift.

- Needless to say, the impact is always negative and becomes increasingly apparent as you get older. Just because you can handle your tasks right now doesn't mean that in 5 or 10 years you'll be able to go on about your life in the same way. And it's always better to cultivate healthy habits early on.

- Multitasking can also impair memory. In 2011, the University of California, San Francisco published a research study showing how quickly shifting from one task to another impacts short-term memory.

- How many times a day do you read or write status updates on your phone? If your thumb is permanently locked in reading news stories on the web the entire day, the rest of you isn't living. Only connecting with your immediate surroundings or interacting fully with other human beings can give you that sense of deep fulfillment.

How to Stop Multitasking

- Do not start your morning by looking at your phone. While you may think a glance at your phone in the morning will not cause any harm, it can be a major drain on your productivity. Checking your phone as soon as you wake up will put you into a reactive state of mind. Wait at least an hour before checking your phone.

- Create a list of daily priorities. Make a list of tasks that you need to complete and list them in the priority that they need to be done. This way, each of your tasks will get your full focus, and you will make sure that the most crucial ones are completed. If you do not get through everything on your list, move those items to the next day.

- Designate time to work on one task or project. Do a project work or go to a meeting room or work location, focus on the task at hand.

- Keep work areas clean and organized. Messed-up things can be distracting. Organize your desk so that you can tackle one thing at a time. You should remove all distracting items that can pull your attention away.

- Be sure to single task during your prime time. You should schedule work that is challenging and requires a lot of focus for the time of day when your attention and drive are at their peak. For example, if you are a morning person, tackle these projects first thing after you get to work. If you attempt to complete these tasks when you are physically or mentally fatigued, it will not be productive.

- Reduce or eliminate outside distractions. Do your best to eliminate distractions throughout the day. Turn off your email, text messages, and social media notifications while you are completing tasks.

- Set a time for distractions. Set a specific time each day to check email, social media, and text messages. This can be your lunch break or a set period before you leave the office.

- Be prepared to say no. Sometimes you may find yourself multitasking because you took on a task you do not have time for. Do not be afraid to say no when asked to complete additional tasks. Be aware of how much is on your plate and how long it will take to complete. If you cannot fit anymore in your day, simply decline. There is no need to provide a long explanation; keep it short and simple.

- Be aware of your multitasking habits. The first step in breaking a habit is being aware of it. If you find yourself constantly multitasking, choose a day to log everything you do so that you can identify patterns that lead to your distractions and be mindful of them in the future.

Chapter Summary

If you are prone to multitasking, this is not a habit you will want to indulge in—it slows you down and decreases the quality of your work. Even if it does not cause brain damage, allowing yourself to multitask will fuel any existing difficulties you have with concentration, organization, and attention to detail.

Sacrifices of Time

*"The journey has definitely not been easy,
but all the sacrifice has paid off very well in
terms of my performance on-court".*
- Rohan Bopanna

We all have 24-hours in a day. But, why are some people able to get the most out of every minute of the day? Do they have the power to slow down or hold the time? No, it never happens. However, many people know how to utilize their time properly in a productive way. We all know how important time is, we all know time flies very fast and once it is gone, nobody in the world has the power to get it back. If you study your spent time thoroughly, you will come to know all the unproductive times, which we do knowingly and unknowingly. Fun and enjoyment eat a big chunk of that. If we can save some of this unproductive time, our productivity will rise steeply.

Hence, success needs the sacrifice of your entertainment time, success asks you to utilize every second of time in a useful and productive way. If you want success then work hard in every second that you get, because every second can change your life and destiny, every second gives you chance to have a new beginning of an era. Hence, never waste your time on something which may give you temporary refreshment it gives you nothing but regret.

How Does It Impact?

There are so many things to do in a day – it is not about having enough time, it is about making productive use of your time. We all have the same 24 hours and we all have the opportunity to use our time productively. When we sacrifice time, we are prioritizing a certain task over another one. Accomplishing that task helps us to reach our goal.

Many people write to-do lists every day and they stick to them. They set their deadlines and try their level best not to procrastinate. Even if they do, they never say that they should have more time. Instead, They set a timeline for the task. Therefore, if you do not productively utilize your time, you will never achieve the bigger goals that are most important to them.

There are 1440 minutes and they took count every minute of their day and thereby, they improve their productivity and efficiency but they lose some good friendships and relationships along the way – that is the price they pay for their success.

How To Make Use of Time

As you make progress along your journey towards your desired outcomes, you need to make difficult choices. Most importantly success demands that you make difficult daily choices about how you spend your time, energy, and money. If you consistently invest your time into meaningful tasks with full focus, you will be slowly moving towards your goal. Spending your time on the less important things takes you away from your goal. This requires that you focus on the right things, at the right time, in the right way and spend just the right amount of time on them.

Most successful people in the world had no time to watch TV, play video games, chit-chat on social media, hang out with friends and family, or pursue their hobbies. They allocate all the precious time for their goals. They worked non-stop for several years sacrificing many things. But, they never regret the sacrifice because they made that choice.

Those successful people sincerely follow the Pareto Principle in personal as well as professional life. The Pareto Principle, also known as the 80-20 rule suggests that 80% of results come from 20% of the efforts put in. To maximize efficiency, highly productive people identify the most important 20% of their work. Then, they look at ways to cut down the other 80% of their schedule, to find more time for the things that make the biggest impact.

Chapter Summary

In nutshell, time is precious cannot be paused. Hence, we need to ensure productive utilization of every second of the day. If we can make use of time by sacrificing entertainment time and other unproductive times, our productivity will increase drastically and chances of getting success will be much higher.

Your ability to manage your time, as much as any other practice in your career will determine your success or failure. Time is one of the indispensable and irreplaceable resources of accomplishment. It is your most precious asset. It cannot be saved, nor can it be recovered once lost. Everything you have to do requires time, and the better you use your time, the more you will accomplish, and the greater will be your rewards.

Sacrifice of Excuse

"He that is good for making excuses is seldom good for anything else"
- Benjamin Franklin

Imagine if Steve Jobs and Steve Wozniak said that for them to start a company they needed an office to start in First and not just a garage. We would not even have Apple today.

Many of us have the habit of giving excuses when we are questioned about our misconduct and failures rather than admitting failure and accepting the responsibility. Making excuses for mistakes is not new. It is the easiest way to defend ourselves and to get temporary relief.

Excuses come into your head to prevent yourself from an upsetting situation, or an excuse to tell someone else because you simply cannot ignore them. The common reasons why people make excuses throughout their lives are fear of failure, fear of uncertainty, lack of purpose or goal, fear of making mistakes, reluctance to take risks, lack of motivation, etc.

Former United States President Theodore Roosevelt came from fantastic New York wealth. But the things that we most associate with his life today are his extraordinary work ethic and his attitude — the vigor and love with which he lived his life.

While Roosevelt benefited from opportunities as a child, he earned everything that he had in his adult life. No one gave him anything. He made sacrifices, read voraciously, created new opportunities, and carved out the life that he envisioned in his dreams. He never made excuses.

What Is The Impact of Making Excuses?

Instead of seeing what we have to do right to capitalize on an opportunity, the habit of making excuses will make you focus only on the negative side, it will make you see what you are lacking and what will make it okay for you not going for your opportunities instead, and this will give you a way to back out of the challenge.

Excuses are harmful because they prevent one from succeeding. When we make excuses and repeat them often enough, they become a belief. The belief then becomes a self-fulfilling prophecy. They attack the belief system by the repetition of excuses.

A sales executive discouraged by his poor sales starts to blame the quality of his product. He keeps on saying that no one wants to buy the product because the quality is not good. After repeatedly making this excuse, he begins to believe it is true. When it attacks the belief system, it halts our progress and thinking pattern and he never comes out from this situation.

Excuses are like stop signs. It prevents the person to own the responsibility. If we are to take credit for our successes, we must assume responsibility for our failures.

By making an excuse, you are taking away an opportunity to succeed, which can limit you in every area of your life. You may never even know what you are capable of if you have an excuse for everything that comes your way. Excuses can hold you back from a lot of things, including limiting progress in your career, getting healthier, and creating new relationships, etc.

Benefits of Sacrifices of Excuse

By refusing to make excuses and embracing responsibility, we reap many rewards. The successes brought by this attitude act as a foundation for self-respect, pride, and confidence. Responsibility breeds competence and power. By living up to our promises and obligations, we win the trust of others. Once we are seen as trustworthy, people will willingly work with us, for our mutual benefits. Therefore, making excuses can put the brakes on our progress, while accepting responsibility can lead us to the top.

How To Stop Making Excuses

Many people believe that opportunities come to certain selected people and not others. If you study those who have become wildly successful, you will find in many instances, many of these people came from nothing and created their opportunities.

- It is necessary to realize that your success or failure depends on you. It depends on the choices you make. It depends on your attitude. You should make a resolution to start accepting responsibility today and do not find an excuse, but find a way. Winston Churchill said, "Responsibility is the price of greatness."

- People make excuses to hide behavior they are ashamed of. When people try to hide their shameful conduct, this is dangerous because they become unaware of what they are doing. However, you can fight this by looking for cues. For instance, if someone challenges your conduct and you become angry, it probably suggests you are guilty as charged.

- From time to time, stop and examine your progress. You should compare where you are now with where you would like to be.

Ask yourself why there is a gap between these two points. You should not make excuses, instead, make plans and take corrective action.

- Take responsibility for your actions and their consequences. When you make a mistake, accept responsibility; learn from it, and move forward. You need to stop making excuses and start taking responsibility for your actions, thoughts, and behaviors.

- When you have a goal in front of you, you will think twice before giving an excuse. So, at least you set short goals.

- Visualization of goals has a motivating power to confront the challenges.

Chapter Summary

If you want to improve any area of life, stop making excuses and blaming others and instead take responsibility for your life and actions and go forward boldly and take charge. Successful people know that they are responsible for their life, no matter their starting point, weaknesses, and past failures. Realizing that you are responsible for what happens next in your life is both frightening and exciting. And when you do, that becomes the only way you can become successful, because excuses limit and prevent us from growing personally and professionally. Every time you give an excuse, it cripples you and kills your chances of success.

Sacrifices of Morning Sleep

"6-7-8 hours of sleep is the game, don't get it twisted- it's not how much you sleep it's what you do while you are awake."
–Gary Vaynerchuk

Do you feel guilty when you get up in the morning for oversleeping? Just think of an answer before moving forward. But when you think, you will find oversleeping is an issue for most of the people who did not succeed or just mediocre.

Why Do We Need Sleep?

Sleep is a part and parcel of life, as it consumes a major portion of your life. Depending on how much you sleep, it constitutes about one-third of all our life. So if you are 30 years old, you have already slept almost 10 years in your 30 years of life span. That is huge. But, just like eating, sleep is necessary for survival. Most adults require between seven to eight hours of sleep. Children and teenagers need substantially more sleep, particularly if they are below five years of age.

Sleep is an essential function that allows your body and mind to recharge, leaving you refreshed and alert when you wake up. Sleep gives your body a rest and allows it to prepare for the next day. It is like giving your body a mini-vacation. Sleep also gives your brain a chance to sort things out. Healthy sleep also helps the body remain healthy and keeps you away from diseases. Without enough sleep, the brain cannot function properly. This can impair your abilities to concentrate, think clearly, and process memories.

Sleep is vital to the rest of the body too. When people don't get enough sleep, their health risks rise. Symptoms of depression, seizures, high blood pressure, and migraines were observed. Sleep also plays a role in metabolism. Even one night of missed sleep can create a prediabetic state in an otherwise healthy person.

Insufficient sleep can lead to serious repercussions. Some studies have shown sleep deprivation leaves people vulnerable to attention lapses, reduced cognition, delayed reactions, and mood shifts. Additionally, lack of sleep has been linked to a higher risk for certain diseases and medical conditions. These include obesity, type 2 diabetes, high blood pressure, heart disease, stroke, poor mental health, and early death.

Why Sleep is Considered a Hindrance To Success?

You must have listened many times in your life where sleep becomes a major hindrance to success. Your parents might have been complaining you of not waking up early, your teachers might have been motivating you to sacrifice sleep for a better result in school and college. You also might have been thinking that you should sleep less and work more. So, everybody including you is against sleep which is probably the only thing in many phases of your life that you truly enjoy. The primary question, "Why sleep and work mostly defined as mutually exclusive or antonyms to each other?"

A Drawback of Less Sleep in Success

Sleep is really important. Sacrificing a few hours will completely mess with your performance on the very next day- especially if you have a job that requires a lot of mental energy. You wouldn't also be able to handle stress correctly.

The problem is that it is not always possible to maintain a perfect sleep regimen. If your schedule allows it, you should alter your sleeping patterns occasionally. Learn to sleep in the day, or stay up all night. There may be times when, in a critical situation, you may be required to stay up for long periods with very little sleep. Allow yourself to experience what that feels like. If you have to do it for real, the shock to your system will at least be a familiar one. If you travel often, as I do, you may become afflicted by jet lag. Use this opportunity to allow your body to learn how to function in unfamiliar patterns.

Sleep is delicious. It's restorative, like a great meal. We need it to survive. But for all adults, there's a line we must draw for where we spend our time. For writers, or anyone pursuing large goals over extended periods, sleep is often an area that can be sacrificed for significant productivity gains.

Why Adequate Sleep is Important for Productive Work

"Sleep is as important as water and food," said Pat Byrne, the founder of Fatigue Science, a company that works with athletes and companies to help them use sleep to increase performance. But many people struggle to prioritize it.

It's hard for people who sleep very little each night to detect the consequences, Byrne said, because after a while their bodies "re-norm" so they can continue to go through the motions during the day, even while they're getting just four or five hours of sleep a night. But that doesn't mean the sleep-deprived person is functioning as well as he or she could be.

"It's very insidious in that it creeps up on you," Byrne said of the effects of a prolonged lack of sleep. That dynamic may explain why executives and others think they are operating just fine on a prolonged lack of sleep.

Successful entrepreneurs sacrifice a good night of sleep to plan for the success of their business. Sleep is a sacrifice that successful people use to make frequently. Sacrificing sleep can unlock more hours in the day for you to do more work and carry out your work.

Should We Sacrifice Our Sleep or Not?

The bottom line is you cannot go without sleep even a single day, unless there is an absolute genuine reason to do so. The way our body is wired would never allow us to do that. Sleep is vital but so is a success. We need to balance where we can get the right amount of both. The truth about sleep regarding success is not that you should sacrifice sleep for success but it's more like "you must be willing sacrifice sleep (in part mostly or completely in a day) whenever success demands". This mindset acknowledges all the beneficial effects of sleep but at the same time it also points out that getting a complete 8 hours or more of sleep every day can come as an obstacle to success and you must choose success at all times if you want it bad enough.

My suggestion is that you intend to sleep normally 7-8 hours every single day. The number itself matters less than what is coming next. It is better to make a long-term plan with fixed hours of sleep, say 8 hours. Treat this as a ritual in sleep that you can execute for years and years to come. Now you have decided the number of hours then that is your maximum. At most means, there could be days when you do not sleep at all but the maximum has to be that number which you decided. This is for the entire week including weekends or holidays. Even if you sleep for the same amount of time every day let's say 8 hours there is a hell of a difference between sleeping from 10 pm to 6 am on one day and sleeping from 2 am to 10 am on the other. This type of inconsistency of schedule should be avoided as far as possible because in such case, even if you completed the schedule 8 hours sleep, you will not feel the freshness. Your body does not like this type of change. Unless you have a genuine reason, nobody values that at all.

Work schedules, day-to-day stressors, a disruptive bedroom environment, and medical conditions can all prevent us from receiving quality sleep. A healthy diet and positive lifestyle habits can help ensure an adequate amount of sleep each night.

Adults who do not receive a sufficient amount of sleep can implement some positive lifestyle and sleep habits. These include the following:

- Establish a routine sleeping time and stick to it every night, even on the weekends.

- Ensure sleep environment is comfortable.

- Abstain from alcohol and large meals in the hours leading up to bedtime.

- Refrain from using tobacco at any time of day or night.

- Exercise during the day; this can help you wind down in the evening and prepare for sleep.

Points To Be Noted:

- The sacrifice of a sleep party for a certain period or completely for a day o meet some urgent requirements is acceptable.

- Oversleeping on an above the stipulated and pre-decided sleeping hours is not acceptable and that is not for health and mind also. You will feel tired when you overslept and your productivity will be dropped.

- Discipline in sleeping time is also to be followed as far as possible which helps to maintain the body clock.

Chapter Conclusion

Sleep is vitally important. Like eating, sleeping is regulated by powerful internal drives. Going without food produces the uncomfortable sensation of hunger while going without sleep makes us feel overwhelmingly sleepy.

But no matter how hard you try to preserve healthy sleeping habits, you're going to sacrifice some sleep to get success. There will be phases in your life in which you have to forgo exactly that. Instead of turning back in the morning, you will have to get up to get to the seminar or the important lecture on time; Instead of scurrying to bed on time in the evening, you will stay at the desk to study for the next exam or to finish your thesis. In the long term, you will find a way to adjust your sleep rhythm and in between, even longer recovery breaks. But in the short term, you'll have to beat one or two short nights around your ears. Otherwise, you will oversleep your studies.

How To Maximize Your Success

"There is no progress or accomplishment without sacrifice."– Idowu Koyenikan

Sacrifice is inevitable to succeed. But it never guarantees success. But, when a person makes a big sacrifice, other success elements such as hard-working, persistence, perseverance, willpower, confidence, risk-taking ability, etc. increases very much. In this chapter, we will try to understand the factors to improve the efficacy of the sacrifice or in other words improve the chances of success.

What Are You Going to Achieve?

In the journey of life, setting goals is the most important thing you can do in your life. Life without goals is like a ship without a rudder, you are directionless and going nowhere. When you know your destination, it is easier to make an action plan to reach there. Goal setting is a powerful process for thinking about your ideal future, and for motivating yourself to turn your vision of this future into reality. Goal setting is fundamental to long-term success, with many short intermediate goals. Establishing a goal creates a sense of clarity and correlation between the process of working hard and accomplishing something significant. The next step is to prepare a proper action plan and implementation of the action to achieve those goals.

When you are in the process of achieving your goals, several challenges crop up. Some of the challenges are very hard, require a lot of time, energy, and hard work. Generally, people allocate time for different activities in life. But when you set some goals with a time frame and you are desperate to achieve that goal, you need to re-allocate more time towards the achievement of goals. You need to allocate more time for these activities. There comes the sacrifice. Before making a sacrifice, you need to make a primary evaluation to get maximum chances of success. But when you are desperate or the purpose is very strong, the decision of sacrifice comes automatically from inside to go all out to achieve what you dreamt.

Understand "Why" of Sacrifices?

A person who can sacrifice is the one who has a purpose and meaning in his life. Sacrifice just for the sake of sacrifices does not fetch any success. The WHY is the biggest driver to success, it creates the desperation to achieve the goal. Therefore, the purpose and the WHY of sacrifice are very important. The bigger the purpose, the easier it to make sacrifices and the greater the chances of success. The purpose drives a person to go all out full of resources for the goal and the success. Great people like Martin Luther King, Winston Churchill, Nelson Mandela, and Mahatma Gandhi always had a purpose in life and had an attitude to sacrifice everything to those purposes. They made all the efforts to accomplish the purpose and had taken all necessary actions to become successful and they became famous in the world. Not only that, you take an example of successful people at any level, you will find their uniqueness in their attitude towards achieving the goal.

Success is not certain even with the best of efforts, but it is true when efforts and sacrifices are made with clear focus and direction, there are maximum chances of success. Even though the sacrifices fail to give the success due to any reason, the regret will be least.

What Should Be The Approach?

If someone wanted to make a change or progress in life, how would they go about it? Everything in life comes as a choice. In many cases, you are just making choice. Like when you decide to spend your time in study instead of chit-chatting with friends, you are choosing that. Similarly, when you decide to excel in a job by spending more time on creative thinking and innovation in work instead of doing a normal routine job and go home.

Shifting your mindset from sacrificing to making choice is essential. When you choose something instead of sacrificing, you are prioritizing your work for the achievement of your goals in your life. Therefore, by shifting the mindset, you look at what you are getting out of your life, rather than what you are missing.

Chapter Summary

Sacrifice just for the sake of sacrifice does not yield results. There should be strong reasons for sacrifice with shifting mindset to choosing life.

Book Summary

"A noble purpose inspires sacrifice, stimulates innovation and encourages perseverance." - Gary Hamel

Success comprises many important elements. Sacrifice is one of the key important element which is always attached with success. Anyone who has accomplished anything worthwhile has never done it without sacrifice. Sacrifice increases self-control avoids distractions and temptations. It means staying focused.

Success requires some kind of sacrifice. You will not gain something for anything. That is not how the world works, and it is therefore certainly not something you can bank on. If you are not willing to make the necessary sacrifices to attain your goals and objectives, the first impact will be that you will not be able to create the momentum you need to get your desired outcomes. This book has clearly described all the elements of sacrifice in the journey to success and its impact on our prosperity. No matter what goals or aspirations you might have, there is one thing certain that you must pay a price to get what you want in life. Any type of success demands something from you. It is simply the way life works and rarely will a shortcut ever get you there.

Nothing worth comes the easy way, least of all business success. Making a sacrifice for success is inevitable. However, be careful not to lose the things that matter and make you happy along the way. You should not realize at the end of the day that the sacrifices for greatness you made cost you happiness, health, and peace. At least the achievement should much bigger than the sacrifices. This book has outlined all the details of very common sacrifices made by successful people.

Success is pure science. Success is not something you get suddenly or just by luck, success is something which you earn, success is something which you achieve by your hard work, success is something which asks for sacrifice, success comes to people who go towards it, it never comes to you on its own in a silver platter.

In a nutshell, your willingness to sacrifice directly determines your level of success—if you only make small sacrifices, you will only achieve small success. If you want to accomplish an enormous goal such as a World-class dancer, you need to make enormous sacrifices. Sacrifice is hard—no one said it would be easy—but every massive success requires massive sacrifice because real success has never been possible without any sacrifices. Many people want to be entrepreneurs, want to build an empire but not everybody can persist to take the thorny road full of mental, physical, and emotional toll with many sacrifices being made along the way.

You must have heard and read many success stories about inspiring entrepreneurs, but in many cases, there is a dark side to achieving a successful outcome. The dark side does not come out in public often. This book has outlined the basic and seven powerful sacrifices which you need to understand properly so that you will consider all aspects mentioned in the book before sacrifice and maximize the chances of attaining success.

"Sacrifice is a part of life. It's supposed to be. It's not something to regret. It's something to aspire to."
— Mitch Albom

Disclaimer

Although the publisher and the author have made every effort to ensure that the information in this book is correct, and while this publication is designed to provide accurate information regarding the subject matter covered, the publisher and the author assume no responsibility for errors, inaccuracies, omissions, or any other inconsistencies herein and hereby disclaim any liability to any party for any loss, damage, or disruption caused by errors or omissions, and whether such errors or omissions result from negligence, accident, or any other cause.

The ideas, procedures, and suggestions in this book are not intended as a substitute for consulting with an expert. Neither the author nor the publisher shall be liable or responsible for any loss or damage allegedly arising from any information or suggestion in this book.

Names, characters, and incidents in this book are either the product of the author's imagination or used in a fictitious manner. Any resemblance to an actual person, living or dead, or actual events is purely coincidental.

COPYRIGHT © 2021 PRADIP N DAS

All rights reserved. No part of this book shall be reproduced or transmitted in any form or by any means, electronic or mechanical, without permission from the author.

Gratitude

This book is dedicated to the Almighty, whose continuous blessings helped me to be an Author.

I sincerely thank all my readers, who inspired me with their love and appreciation for my previous books.

Jn

www.ingramcontent.com/pod-product-compliance
Lightning Source LLC
LaVergne TN
LVHW020344200726
843507LV00012B/2489